ABERDEEN AND BEYOND

AT WORK AND PLAY

Shift change at Kemnay Quarry in 1946.

Top right, fish quines at Aberdeen Harbour in the 1930s.

ABERDEEN
AND BEYOND

AT WORK AND PLAY

Raymond Anderson

BLACK & WHITE PUBLISHING

First published 2010
by Black & White Publishing Ltd,
29 Ocean Drive, Edinburgh EH6 6JL

1 3 5 7 9 10 8 6 4 2   10 11 12 13

ISBN: 978 1 84502 319 5

Typeset by www.richardbudddesign.co.uk
Printed and bound by MPG Books Ltd, Bodmin, Cornwall

The photographs drawn from *The Press and Journal* archives can be purchased
from The Photosales Department.
Tel: 01224 338011, or by visiting www.photoshopscotland.com

CONTENTS

Farmers strike a deal at Aberdeen Feein' Market in the 1930s.

ACKNOWLEDGEMENTS

My thanks to Duncan Smith, Russell Morrison, Iain Tavendale,
Bob Stewart and Susan Mckay who each in their own way played an important
part in bringing this book to publication.

Highland Games legend Bill Anderson launches the stone at the Aboyne Games in 1960.

INTRODUCTION

INTRODUCTION

ONCE again the photographic archive of Aberdeen Journals is opened up.

This is the sixth book in a series stretching back to Images of Aberdeen, which was published in 1994. I am pleasantly surprised that we have managed to fill so many books. But considering that *The Press and Journal* was providing news for the area ninety-two years before the invention of photography, it is perhaps not so strange that there is so much to share.

As the title *Aberdeen and Beyond* suggests, the countryside surrounding the city gets more prominence in this book. That is only proper as it is especially the sea to our east and the farmlands to north, south and west which shaped the character of the people who wrestled a livelihood from those two harsh masters – ocean and soil.

In this book, romantic scenes of Clydesdales pulling ploughs along sunlit farmlands jostle for attention with pictures that show all too vividly how harsh a North-east winter can be.

Some scenes seem to be from another world rather than another time. The Feein' Market so much a part of the country folk's life at one time is graphically recorded in this book. Working men, and women, being, in effect, bought along the roadside seems alien to us today. But this practice continued until the disruptions of the Second World War changed society forever.

Lost trades and long gone buildings also feature in this look at our past. Cobbled streets and narrow alleys are recalled. And some might ponder whether some of the buildings that replaced them were indeed such an improvement. In the twenty-first century, constructions from the brave new world of the Sixties can look but a temporary aberration.

But the North-east has always had the great benefit of having one of nature's best building materials to hand. Granite made Aberdeen what it is today – on the best days, a sparkling and solid city. Even on the bleak days, granite imparts a grandeur that other cities can only aspire to.

The granite industry, which once was such a part of Aberdeen and surrounding areas, most notably Kemnay, has a fascinating tale to tell. And the pictures of the hey-day of that great industry are truly dramatic.

Royalty too plays its part in this book. No record of the North-east could be compiled without them, particularly a record that includes the more deferential Fifties.

The great celebrations of country life are well represented. The Highland Show, the Aboyne Games and, of course, the Braemar Gathering. Glancing through the pictures, I was surprised to realise that they nearly all bask in sunshine.

But we know the weather is not always benign in the North-east and the great blizzards of the late 1950s and early 1960s provide dramatic pictures of trains, lorries and people trapped.

We are always at the mercy of Mother Nature, but perhaps not so much now as in those days when manual labour was used to dig out trapped trains and vehicles.

The huge changes wrought by the youth revolution are also recorded as fashion and attitudes changed forever.

The selection of subjects is as random as the diary of the news and picture editors, who over the decades sent reporters and photographers out to document the everyday events, both trivial and momentous, which made up daily life in North-east Scotland.

The names of these experts of their trade were all too often not recorded but prominent among the photographers we do know are Gordon Bissett, Charles Flett, John Gallicker and Ian Hardie. We owe these, and all the un-named, a debt of gratitude for recording life in our corner of the world with a skill and sensitivity born of a deep knowledge and love of our country.

Two Clydesdales lean into their work as a farmer ploughs a field with Aberdeen spread out below. Prominent in this pre-high flats scene is the Bridge of Dee and to the left of the picture, above the Richards Ltd buildings by the River Dee, is the ice rink that once stood on South Anderson Drive. The site fell into disuse after the Second World War, during which a Nazi plane pursued by the RAF crashed into the building. Part of the site is now the Headland Court housing development.

MAN'S HELPERS

Ploughing with a pair of horses in 1962.

CHAPTER ONE

MAN'S HELPERS

THE bond between working horses and their handlers is a special one. In today's machinery-dominated world, it is hard to conceive that brief generations ago the horse was a vital part of the world of work.

The expression "willing workhorse" was never more apt than on the farms. In the pages that follow, we see the many uses that horses were put to. For anything that needed hauled, a horse was called into service. Whether it was to pull a load of hay or the more skilled teaming of man and horse to produce a straight furrow.

The care and attention lavished on these animals is reflected in the special attention men took in fitting out their charges in gleaming collars and harnesses for shows.

Of course it was not just on the farm that the horse was needed. As recently as the 1950s, the British Railways' Aberdeen stud had eighty-nine animals. The pride workers took to present these magnificent animals in all their finery shines through in our images from a carthorse competition of 1951.

The farmer's lonely toil with his horses is captured in this striking study.

A ploughman holds a
steady course as he fashions
out a straight drill.

Four teams of horses harrow
a field, breaking up clods of
earth and covering the seeds
for the next harvest.

Horses wait patiently
with their carts for
the next load.

Ploughmen at work
in North-east Scotland
in 1950.

North-east farmers took
great pride in marrying
the power of their horses
to the strength and skill of
the ploughmen. Here men
compete to produce the
straightest furrows.

A horse with a device for
sowing seeds is followed by
a team of horses harrowing
over the seeds.

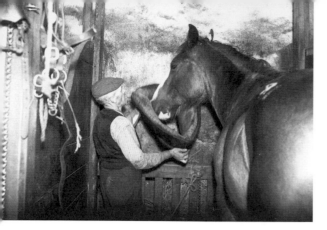

A farm horse gets its collar fitted in 1945.

A horse harness is lovingly burnished by a ploughman in 1948.

A saddler skillfully
fashions a horse collar.

Horses in harness compete for show honours in 1948.

Clydesdales are proudly displayed in their best show finery.

The first Aberdeen goods-station horse parade at Guild Street, Aberdeen, in 1951. On show were seventeen specially selected horses from the British Railways' Aberdeen stud of eighty-nine animals. They were competing for the honour of being chosen as the city's best-kept carthorse. The horses were back between the shafts the following Monday but one horse – Tommy, a dark brown eight-year-old – had a gold medallion pinned to his harness. As winner of the Aberdeen event, he went on to compete at the Royal Highland Show.

Some of the many men who worked to keep horses at work in the towns and on the farms. Blacksmiths at work preparing shoes in 1938.

Something a bit different. A bullock is shoed in the 1930s.

A farrier at work shoeing a horse at West North Street, Aberdeen, in 1963.

Jim Johnston pictured
in the Fintray smiddy,
Aberdeenshire, in 1971.

The ever-inventive North-east farmer didn't need to have horses to run out a drill. Here a ploughman is using oxen.

Hoeing by hand on a North-east farm in the 1930s.

Preparing the soil for the sowing on a North-east Scotland farm in late May 1967.

A field of straight furrows at a ploughing match with horses on land beside Kincardine O'Neil on Deeside.

William Still,
Burnhead
of Clinterty,
sharpening
his scythe
before tackling
another
stretch of
barley in 1948.

HAIRST

Swinging the scythe in a field. This worker is cutting
what was termed a "road".

CHAPTER TWO

HAIRST

THE gathering in of the harvest is a special time on farms everywhere. And here we have all the different aspects of the hairst, from the sharpening of the scythe to the hayricks and the threshing.

But it wouldn't be the North-east if the weather didn't take a hand and we also record the struggles to salvage something of the harvest after the downpours and floods of 1956.

Here again our pictures span the age when the harvest was gathered by man and horse through to the era when combine harvesters, however primitive, began to revolutionise farming.

Making the gathering of the harvest a slightly less backbreaking job with a harvesting machine and tractor in the North-east in 1962.

One of the early
tractors harvesting
in ideal weather.

An International
tractor harvesting with
Bennachie, near Inverurie,
as a backdrop.

Haymaking on Deeside in 1961. The old Crathie cemetery, where Queen Victoria's servant John Brown is buried, is in the background with Victoria's monument to Prince Albert prominent on the hill beyond.

Not all harvests go smoothly. In 1956, floods wreaked havoc. Here workers try to salvage what they can after the River Dee burst its banks.

The sun shines on a farmer during harvesting at Dalmaik Farm, Drumoak, Aberdeenshire, in 1965.

A woman lends a hand to save as much of the 1956 harvest as possible after bad flooding on Deeside.

Ideal harvesting weather at Dalmaik Farm, Drumoak, in late August 1965.

A welcome cup of tea as workers and horses take a break during a North-east harvest in the 1930s.

Children hitch a ride as a horse hauls the hay home in July 1938.

Men and horses at work in the fields at harvest time.

A dog leads the way for the horse team during harvesting on Deeside.

A horse-drawn harvester works its way through a field as men stack hayricks.

Threshing work in 1966 with the Bridge of Dee and Aberdeen city in the background.

A steam traction engine powers a threshing machine. These steam machines took an increasing role in farming and industry from the middle of the nineteenth century until well into the early part of the twentieth century.

The arrival of the threshing machine is a good excuse for all the workers to gather around for a photograph to mark that most auspicious of days in the harvest season.

Time for a welcome rest during the harvesting. Some mechanisation has arrived but the toil remains hard.

Combine harvesters at work at Castle Fraser, Aberdeenshire, in September 1961.

A shepherd in a snowdrift shields a lamb from the worst of a raw day in the North-east.

WORKING THE LAND

A picture postcard scene perhaps, but the beauty of new-fallen snow comes at a price for shepherds with everything becoming a little harder and harsher. This picture was taken in 1954 at Park, Aberdeenshire.

CHAPTER THREE

WORKING THE LAND

THE countryside has always played a huge part in defining the character of the North-east of
Scotland. In this selection of pictures from the past we see the harshness as well as the beauty
of lives lived in a landscape that can be benign or malign . . . often in the same day.

The ancient ways of the shepherd are represented as are the technological changes that
have transformed farming. It's interesting to note that as early as 1962 helicopters were being
used for crop spraying in the North-east.

The turn of the year 1959
with sheep taken down
from the hills for shelter.

Lambing season 1960 and
a proud shepherd shows
off the new arrivals.

Sheep returning from the hills
to lowland winter feeding
in the Glens of Foudland
between Inverurie and Huntly
in November 1946.

Sheep on the Keith to Huntly road in the 1940s.

Hand shearing sheep on
an Aberdeenshire farm.

Turkeys on display as Christmas draws nearer.

Feathers getting ruffled as geese go on the move.

"Shepherding" geese at a North-east farm.

The turkey trot with a dog, beside the tree, getting in on the act.

Two cattlemen with a Highland bull in the 1940s.

Farm workers planting potatoes by hand.

The neatly ploughed fields at Tullynessle, near Alford, are framed by trees in this study.

Highland cattle at Douneside, Tarland.

Cattle in a new covered court at North Ythsie, Aberdeenshire, in 1950.

Waiting patiently for the water cart at an Aberdeenshire farm during the hot summer of 1947.

Milking cows by hand in Aberdeenshire.

A girl gets to grips with milking by hand in 1957.

A champion white pig is taken into its pen.

A helicopter is prepared before it takes off to spray crops in 1962.

The helicopter in action, crop spraying at Brimmond Hill, west of Aberdeen.

A nervous Shetland pony is coaxed on to a Danish Air Line freight plane for transportation to Denmark.

Magic Glen, one of the horses trained by John Sorrie at his Inverurie stables. Picture taken in 1962.

Enterprising farmer John Sorrie of Inverurie, in May 1962, with some of the turkeys which he was renowned for.

Precautions to stop the
spread of foot and mouth.

More precautions to ensure the North-east foot and
mouth outbreak did not spread.

Paths were closed in areas
struck by foot and mouth
disease in North-east
Scotland in 1960.

The foot and mouth outbreak in December 1960 sent shockwaves throughout the North-east. Here the Aberdeen Mart is chemically cleansed.

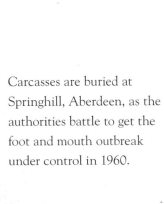

Work underway burying carcasses at Springhill, Northfield, Aberdeen, during the 1960 foot and mouth outbreak.

Carcasses are buried at Springhill, Aberdeen, as the authorities battle to get the foot and mouth outbreak under control in 1960.

Sorting out the tatties. Potato grading underway
at Aberdeen Seed Potato Organisation Ltd of
Potterton, Aberdeenshire, in 1981.

Expert eyes assess a bull at the Kittybrewster
Mart, Aberdeen, in 1965.

Avid interest at the Kittybrewster Mart in 1986.

The cattle sales underway at Belmont
Mart, Aberdeen, in 1971.

A gamekeeper with a grouse bagged on the first day of the new shooting season in 1955.

A grouse hunting party spreads out across Dinnet Moor on the Glorious Twelfth of August 1954.

School dinners in Inverurie in 1962. The canteen at Inverurie Academy, which had many pupils living in the countryside, had to feed 600 pupils in relays daily.

The woman who is a crucial part in the history of the Gordon Highlanders is recreated at the Aboyne Games in 1960. Duchess Jean, wife of the 4th Duke of Gordon, is said to have offered a kiss to any man joining her husband's regiment when it was raised in 1794. First named the 100th Regiment of Foot and then the 92nd, it officially became "The Gordon Highlanders" in 1881. Alongside "Duchess Jean" in the picture are the Marquess and Marchionesss of Huntly.

GATHERING OF THE CLANS

Games heavy, A. Sutherland of Ardross, prepares to release the
hammer at Aboyne in 1960.

CHAPTER FOUR

GATHERING OF THE CLANS

NO record of country life would be complete without the big agricultural shows and the Highland Games.

The sheer scale of the 1951 Royal Highland Show in Aberdeen is impressive, a timely reminder to town dwellers of the importance of the farming industry.

The Highland Games, however, are a celebration of culture rather than commerce. From caber tossing to dancing and piping, a good games will tell much about the Highlander.

We must delve back into the mists of time for the beginnings of the Highland Games. Back to the days when the clan system prevailed and chieftains summoned their clansmen. These gatherings of the clans included military training, and inevitably men tested their strength and speed against each other.

Over the centuries, these tests of strength and skill developed into the Highland Gatherings as we know them. Events largely unchanged since the 1820s.

After raising the Stewart standard at Braemar on 6 September 1715, the 24th Earl of Mar's Highland army marched to camp at Aboyne. Those thousands of men in battle gear must have made that day in September the most memorable of all Aboyne Gatherings.

Similarly, the thousands of Highlanders gathered for the ill-fated raising of the standard for a Jacobite uprising were part of a most remarkable Braemar Gathering. The grand hunt in the Forest of Mar that preceded the standard raising – and was used as a pretext to gather Jacobite lairds together – was part of a tradition believed to date back to the eleventh century. These days-long assemblies also included the strength and skill challenges that became the basis of today's Gatherings.

The direct roots of today's Braemar Gathering go back to 1815 and a society formed to help the poor and needy. The Braemar Highland Society provided money for prizes at the 1832 Gathering and thereafter organized the yearly event. It was in 1848 that Queen Victoria chose to make an appearance at the Gathering and forged a Royal link that lasts to this day.

In the following pages we portray the elements that give the Highland Games their enduring charm – the tradition, the spectacle and the drama.

A general view of the Aboyne Highland Games in 1960.

The crowd keeps warm
at the Royal Braemar
Gathering in 1960.

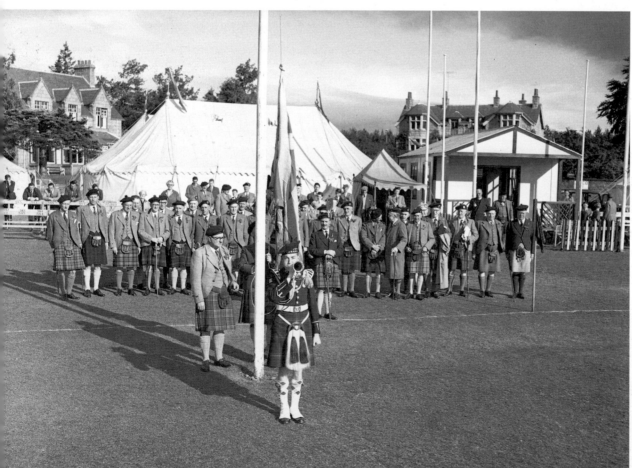

Raising the Standard at the
Aboyne Games in 1960.

Henry Gray throwing the hammer at the Braemar Gathering in 1960.

Farmer and games legend Bill Anderson shows the awesome power that made him such a successful heavy on the circuit. Here he is throwing the stone at the 1960 Aboyne Games. On this occasion he broke two records in events – records he had set himself the previous year. The then twenty-three-year-old from Banchory-Devenick took the Dinnie Trophy and the Dyce Nicol Gold Medal for best in heavy events.

Enjoying the sun and the spectacle at the 1960 Aboyne Games.

Hold it! One of the armed forces tug o' war teams at the Braemar Gathering in 1960 is set up for the big pull.

The 4/7th Gordon Highlander tug o' war team takes the strain on the rope at the 1960 Braemar Gathering.

Catriona Buchanan shows her prize-winning style at the Aboyne Games, 1960.

Champion dancer J. L. McKenzie of Aberdeen collects his silverware at the 1960 Aboyne Games.

Recovering after an exhausting race.

A runner gives his all as he races across the line at the 1960 Aboyne Games.

Three piping experts sit in judgment at the pibroch competition during the 1960 Braemar Gathering

Arms flung back in front of a huge crowd, runners cross the line in the 100-yard sprint at the 1960 Braemar Gathering.

Massed crowds and massed pipe bands at Braemar in 1960.

Aberdeen City Police Pipe Band swing across the main stadium at the 1960 gathering in Braemar.

Under the banner. The Marquess and Marchioness of Huntly arrive in style at the 1960 Aboyne Games.

Aberdeen Angus are judged at the
Royal Highland Show at Hazlehead,
Aberdeen, in 1951. The breed, which
was first produced in Aberdeenshire,
is famous throughout the world.

Innes of Learney judging
costumes at the Aboyne
Games of 1960.

An aerial view showing the size of the 112th Royal Highland Show, which was held at Aberdeen in 1951. At that time it was the largest Royal Highland ever.

The main show ring is prominent in this aerial view of the Royal Highland Show at Aberdeen in June 1951. It was the fourteenth time the great agricultural event had been held in the city.

The Feein' Market at the Castlegate, Aberdeen, on 24 May 1935. More popularly known in the city as Muckle Friday, it was held on a fine sunny day and attracted the largest gathering of farmers and farm servants for many years. But it was one of the last Muckle Fridays, as an increasing number of jobs were being filled through adverts in the local papers like *The Press and Journal*. On this occasion it was reported that farmers were unwilling to commit themselves due to a "mixed outlook in several branches of the agricultural industry". Consequently, quite a large number of men remained unengaged. It is poignant to note that with the cataclysm of the Second World War just a few years away, a piper from Castlehill Barracks is entertaining the crowd while recruiting sergeants mix with the crowd. *The Press and Journal* reported, "Kenspeckle figures in the crowd were the recruiting officers with their gay red, white and blue ribbons flying from their caps and glengarries."

MUCKLE FRIDAY

A large crowd of men are addressed by an Army officer at the 1935 Muckle Friday at Aberdeen's historic Castlegate. The men seeking employment are all dressed in suits and ties for this special day and few are without a "bunnet".

CHAPTER FIVE

MUCKLE FRIDAY

FEEIN' markets were an integral part of life in Scottish market towns from the eighteenth century into the twentieth century.

These employment fairs were held to engage farm workers and took place in May and November, although individual markets adopted their own character dictated by the demand for workers and the particular skills required. Hence, this extract from the *Mearns Leader* newspaper of February 1897:

> The annual feeing market for married farm-servants was held in the Market Square, Stonehaven, last week. The attendance of both farmers and farm-servants was very large. Feeing was stiff, and new engagements were not so profitable in the monetary sense to the servants. The following were the rates of the wages: Foremen and ploughmen with charge, from £27 to £88 per annum, with the usual perquisites; others from £25 to £27.

When a deal was struck for employment, the contract was sealed with a payment. So the market, and the nearby hotels and pubs, did a good trade as the new employees celebrated.

In May 1863, the *Peterhead Sentinel* reported thus:

> The summer feeing market was held at Longside yesterday. Engagements were very stiff and wages had a downward tendency. Winter wages were the rule. Ploughmen (foremen) £10 10s. to £11 10s. Common Ploughmen £9 to £10. Orra Men £6 to £7 10s. Halflins £2 10s. to £4. Boys £2 to £2 10s. Women (first class) £4 10s. to £5. Women (second class) £3 to £4.

Halflins are young men, from the Scots word for not fully grown. An orra man is a spare or extra worker but one couldn't presume to speculate on the difference between a "first class" and "second class" woman.

It seems that this ritual, which many would see as demeaning today, was an eagerly anticipated meeting place and, in good times when employment was plentiful, a popular social gathering.

A farmer tries to strike a deal outside Aberdeen Town House during a pre-war Feein' Market.

Young and old get together at this 1937 Feein' Market in Aberdeen.

Spot the soldiers amid the crowd at this pre-war Feein' Market crowd on Castle Street, Aberdeen.

A country cobbler, clay pipe clamped in his mouth, repairs shoes.

THE CRAFTS FOLK

A cobbler at work on a new pair of shoes
at the Aberdeen premises of Milne and
Munro, Aberdeen, in 1936.

CHAPTER SIX

THE CRAFTS FOLK

IN this section, we celebrate the craftsmen and women who have all but disappeared. Like the cobblers and coopers that are becoming increasingly rare.

A consequence of this change has been the loss of a number of shops that many people will remember with affection.

The weavers, once such a vital part of our society that they were celebrated in song and verse, are also increasingly part of a dying trade. However, one area in the North-east is keeping alive the ancient skill of lace making.

In these days of throwaway shoes it's fascinating to look back to 1965 when repair shops were much in demand and needed large staffs. The Northern Co-op, pictured here, was one of the largest at that time with seventeen hands, but before the Second World War, the company needed a staff of sixty.

Some old-style boots photographed in 1966. The sturdy "tackety beets" were favoured by workmen and often shod the feet of boys and youths. The button boots were a fashion item in their day.

A watchful eye is kept on young shoemaker Kenny Hutcheon in 1966 as he stands amid shoe lasts for individual customers. H. Charles Caie entered the shoemaker craft of the Seven Incorporated Trades of Aberdeen as a "maker" sixteen years earlier. He is thought to have been the last man to do so. In past times, the cordiners' craft was closely regulated in Aberdeen. No "made" work was allowed to be imported into the town, but in return for this protection from outside competition, every part of the craftsmen's lives was controlled by rules. These even extended to the saying of prayers on the Sabbath and attendance at fellow craftsmen's funerals. By 1966, Mr Caie's main work was making surgical boots and dancing shoes.

Eric Munro examines a shoe last in 1966. Behind him are the lasts from which customers' shoes are made. For over a century the principal of Milne and Munro made all the lasts. Mr Eric Munro was the son of James Munro who took over the well-regarded shop, founded in 1849 by James Milne. He specialised in making waterproof leather boots in the days before rubber. The original shop was at the junction of Broomhill Road and Holburn Street, virtually in the country in those days. In 1863, the founder was joined in the business by his son-in-law Andrew Munro. A shop was opened in George Street in 1867. After other moves around central Aberdeen, the firm settled at 263 Union Street in 1901. Many of the shoes sold were made on the Union Street premises by a team of half-a-dozen shoemakers. Aberdonians of a certain age will remember the shop's golden boot sign and also the floor-to-ceiling aviary that delighted youngsters.

Church and Co of Northampton took over the business in 1967. Unfortunately, soaring rates, exacerbated by the oil boom years in the 1970s and changing attitudes towards shoe buying, saw the shop close.

Shoemaker Willie Reid of Aberdeen at work making a pair of shoes surrounded by the tools of his trade in 1966. When this picture was taken, Willie had recently won a diploma of merit in a world competition for shoe repairers.

Jackson Simpson at work on fine detail while renovating an old painting. Mr Simpson was much admired in North-east Scotland for his artistic skill. He started his working life as a lithographer and only seriously took to painting after a distinguished Army career in which he won the Military Cross. He became well known for his watercolours and etchings of views around the North-east. Using his talent as a draughtsman, Mr Simpson produced illustrations for medical teams in the early days of X-ray at Aberdeen Royal Infirmary, Foresterhill.

A bootmaker at Ellon. This picture was taken in October 1946.

David Duncan Senior and Junior at work in Finzean sawmill's turning shop in 1964 where articles like brush handles and parts for golf clubs were made.

Bottling beer at Aberdeen's Devanha Brewery in December 1942. The Devanha Brewery has a long history. A brewery bearing that name was established in 1803 by William Black in a former paper mill beside the Wellington suspension bridge. The brewery's most popular product was Devanha Porter. This dark brown bitter brew became sought after throughout Scotland and England. William Black and Company ran the business until 1910, after which it was taken over by Ushers of Edinburgh but only used as a bottling plant for Ushers' own beers and as a distribution centre.

The bucket mill at Finzean with some of its high-quality buckets. As well as the bucket mill, there is an integrated sawmill and turning mill. These mills on the River Feugh are the only ones of their kind in Scotland still within their original native pinewood forests and still producing their traditional wooden products. Birse Community Trust now owns the sawmill and the turning mill site and is dedicated to the restoration and continued operation of the mills. This picture dates from 1964 when William Brown, grandson of founder Peter Brown, still constructed the tubs from Canadian cedar wood and from Scots Pine. Peter Brown came to the area in 1853.

Pipes being produced at the Cruden Bay Brick and Tile works near Aberdeen in 1947. It was one of the longer lasting of a number of clay pipe and brick making businesses that sprang up in and around Aberdeen in the nineteenth century. The Cruden Bay works started in 1902 supplying millions of bricks for building throughout the nation. In Aberdeen, Richards' Broadford Works was built with Cruden Bay bricks.

Taking newly-fired drainage pipes out of the kiln in 1961.

Bricks are wheeled out of the large coal firing ovens at the Cruden Bay brick works in 1947. The works were linked to the rail network and covered a large area. A nearby quarry supplied the clay for the bricks, drainage pipes and tiles produced here. In the mid-1970s, the factory was working flat out producing 60,000 bricks a week but a decade later, the challenge of newer materials and foreign competition proved too much and the works closed. In 2007, there were plans for almost 200 homes to be built on the old site.

Clay pipes ready for distribution are stacked at the Cruden Bay works in 1961.

Giant cranes form a backdrop for a new ship being fitted out at Hall Russell in 1963 when the shipyard was a major employer in the city.

A welder at work as a new vessel rises between the stocks at the Hall Russell shipyard in Footdee. This was in 1963.

The lunchtime rush through the gates of the Hall Russell shipyard, Aberdeen, in 1963.

Men stacking peat at New Pitsligo in 1971. The peat moss at this Aberdeenshire village was a valuable source of employment for the men of the area for many years.

Gas meters are checked by a workman in 1935.

THE WEAVERS

A complex weaving machine is tended at Broadford Works, Aberdeen, in 1947.

Working at making tweed with the traditional method.

A man with a handful of bobbins at the Keith woollen mills in 1947.

Spinning wool for tweed.

Close attention to weaving detail at the Seafield Mills, Keith, in 1962.

Keeping a close eye on
a weaving machine at
Broadford Works.

Girls at work weaving
at Aberdeen's Broadford
Works in 1949.

A spinning machine at the
Richards Ltd Broadford
Works in the 1960s.

A fine cloth takes shape
at Grandholm Mills,
Aberdeen, in the 1950s.

A final touch is added
to the products of a
woollen mill at Keith.

LACE MAKING

LACE making in New Pitsligo can be traced back to the eighteenth century. Families that fled to the Continent during the 1745 rebellion returned to Britain and brought with them the ancient Flanders lace-making skills. The women of Devon were particularly accomplished lace makers. Then, one account says, early in the nineteenth century, a laird living in the New Pitsligo area visited the south coast and decided to introduce the women of the North-east to lace making.

Two ladies were brought north to teach the art and the seed of a cottage industry was planted. In 1846, the village got a new minister, the Rev. W. Webster. Along with his wife, he took an active interest in the lace making and secured fine thread to replace the more coarse threads used at that time. Tuition helped raise the quality of work to a high standard.

New patterns were designed by the women and the fame of New Pitsligo lace spread. A high point was achieved when Queen Victoria's daughter, Princess Louise, used the lace on her wedding gowns.

The thriving New Pitsligo Lace Club continues to keep this tradition alive in the village. Sheila Joss, who has run the classes since 1981, says: "We're more active than ever. Last year we had twenty adults and ten children. This year we'll have more. They come from all around the village and from as far away as Aberdeen."

Some of the patterns from the New Pitsligo lace makers.

The old skill of lace making lives on in this New Pitsligo house in 1961.

A sharp eye and nimble fingers are required by the New Pitsligo lace makers. It is the tradition that New Pitsligo lace is made with wooden bobbins on a pillow.

OTHER WORK

A wheelwright at work on a wheel hub.

Some of the papermaking machines in operation at Culter Mills in the 1950s.

A rug maker at work in 1936.

An aerial view of the Culter paper mills in 1948. The site is now a housing estate. This huge Culter enterprise that grew up alongside the Culter Burn started in a small way in 1751. The company was never slow to invest in new technology and by 1890, with Culter Paper Mills Co Ltd in charge, the business was producing sixty tons of paper a week. By 1897, a tramway ran between the mill and Culter railway station. The company reached its zenith in the 1950s with more than 600 employees working on a thirty-five-acre site. The mills closed and were demolished in 1981 and the site was developed for housing.

A paper-making machine at Mugiemoss Mills, Bucksburn, in the 1950s. The company, originally C. Davidson and Sons, a reliable source of jobs in the area for 200 years, finally closed down in 2005.

Britain's most northerly coal mine at Brora. Remarkably, the first coal was found on the seashore here in 1529 and mining continued until 1974. On the instructions of the Countess of Sutherland, a "bell-pit" mine was opened in 1598. Over the decades and centuries that the mine expanded, miners came from Cornwall and Wales to add their skills to the dangerous work. After fire and flooding, the Brora mine closed in 1960. But that wasn't the end of this extraordinary venture. The miners themselves took control of the mine and, with the help of the Highland Fund, mining continued for another fourteen years. The site has now been landscaped.

COAL AND ROSES

Men at work filling moulds with molten metal at an iron foundry in March 1939.

CHAPTER SEVEN

COAL AND ROSES

THE diversity of work across the North and North-east of Scotland is reflected in this section. Here we see the men who poured the molten metal and hewed coal from deep in the earth, alongside the very different skills of those who created beautiful roses and the confectionery that so many of us found too tempting to resist.

Women at the John E Esslemont sweet factory in Aberdeen in 1968. It was in that year that the old established firm – it had celebrated its centenary just four years earlier – moved its confectionery and tea blending operations to a new factory at Woodside, Aberdeen. The firm, which began as a corner shop on King Street and Castle Street, was supplying teas and sweets to wholesalers all over Scotland and northern England, and also to Ireland, Canada and the United States. The company was acquired by Bassetts, the Liquorice Allsorts company, in 1973.

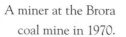

A miner at the Brora coal mine in 1970.

An iron-moulding foundry in March 1939.

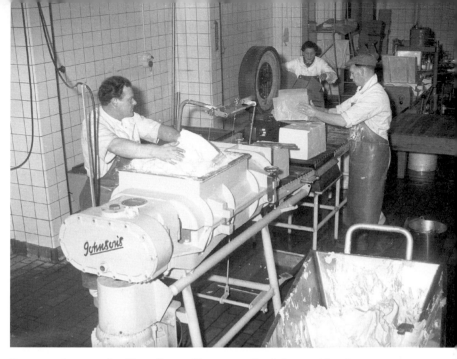

Butter making at the Twin Spires Creamery, Bucksburn, Aberdeen.

Grafting roses in Aberdeen in 1947. On the right is Bob Harper, nursery foreman at James Cocker and Sons for many years.

Workers on the production line at Baxter's of Speyside in Fochabers, Moray.

Distillery
vats pictured
in 1948.

WATER OF LIFE

Cooper Billy Johnston at work producing whisky casks for Glenfiddich Distillery, Dufftown, in April 1962.

CHAPTER EIGHT

WATER OF LIFE

THE details of the happy accident that brought the secrets of whisky distillation to Scotland are long forgotten. But what we do know is that, by the Middle Ages, a raw, rough distilled liquid was being produced here.

The word whisky comes from the Gaelic uisge beatha or "water of life". Speyside, with its plentiful supply of barley and clear streams, could have been specially created for the whisky industry. The area has almost half of Scotland's distilleries and produces outstandingly distinctive whiskies that have devotees around the world. Names like Balvenie, The Macallan, Glenfiddich and Glenlivet have become bywords of excellence.

And what an industry it is, with ninety per cent of its production going overseas and sales running at £2.5 billion a year. The United States and France jostle with each other for the top spot in export markets, each spending well in excess of £400 million a year. Spain, South Korea and Venezuela make up the top five. China's appetite for the water of life rose from sales of just £1 million in 2000 to £80 million in 2009. The whisky industry was worth an annual £3.13 billion to the Scottish economy in 2009 and provides almost 41,000 jobs in Scotland.

Dufftown lays claim to being the Malt Whisky Capital of Scotland. It was famously said that while Rome was built on seven hills, Dufftown was built on seven stills. That figure has varied over the years. The number of distilleries was indeed nine at one time before mothballing and demolition reduced the number. In this 1962 picture, the vat at Dufftown Distillery is checked by a worker. As this is written, six distilleries at Dufftown continue to produce some of the very finest malt whiskies.

Apprentice coopers at a Speyside cooperage. The tradition of blackening barrel-making apprentices was an initiation rite in this trade as in many others. This picture was taken in 1993.

Stillman William Stuart surveys the great copper stills at Glen Keith Distillery in 1962. Glen Keith was opened in 1959 as "twin" to the historic Milton Distillery, which is better known as Strathisla, founded in 1786. Currently owned by Pernod Ricard, the Glen Keith Distillery was mothballed in 2000.

Worker Alex Ross in the grain loft at Banff Distillery in 1962. This much-rebuilt distillery finally closed its doors and was demolished in 1983.

Barrels of whisky are moved at the Balvenie Scotch whisky distillery in Dufftown in 1973. On one side, the 1972 distillation is stored, with 1969 on the other side. The distillery was built in 1892 and remains under the ownership of William Grant and Sons.

The massive maintenance shop for main line diesel locomotives at Inverurie Loco Works.

TRANSPORT

Foreman blacksmith at Inverurie Loco Works David Robertson, right, discusses
a job with one of the blacksmiths in 1962.

CHAPTER NINE

TRANSPORT

IT was the railways that made Inverurie. Before the Great North of Scotland Railway laid track through the hamlet on its way to Huntly, it was Oldmeldrum that was the market town of the area.

That was in 1856, when the Inverurie railway station faced the Kintore Arms Hotel.

But the growing community's reliance on the rail industry was not sealed until 1903, when the Great North of Scotland Railway (GNSR) built its main workshops in Inverurie.

For the following sixty-five years, the Loco Works was an integral part of the town and a vital source of employment. And when the axe did fall, Inverurie reeled and house prices tumbled. As the Loco Works hooter sounded for the last time, the livelihood of some 500 men went, even after the large-scale rundown that had taken place at the site.

Sparks fly, making an impressive picture, as workers fashion metal into material for the huge locomotives assembled and repaired at Inverurie.

Men at work in the Loco Works blacksmith shop in 1962.

The end of trams in Aberdeen. The burned wreckage of the city's last trams are cut up for scrap metal at the Queen's Links on 13 May 1958.

The Aberdonian train service with the Blue Peter steam locomotive on its last run from Aberdeen on 21 August 1957. This A2 Pacific engine was named after the 1939 Derby winner rather than the children's television programme.

The Aberdonian steams out of Aberdeen Joint Station for the last time in 1957. Built in 1948, it spent most of its working life travelling between Aberdeen, Edinburgh and Dundee. In 1951, 60532 reached 100mph in time trials between Montrose and Stonehaven. It was withdrawn from service in 1966 and was featured on the Blue Peter programme. The locomotive was popular on rail tours until 2003. Blue Peter then went on display at Darlington Railway Museum until 2007, when it moved to Barrow Hill Engine Shed in Darlington.

The footbridge over the railway lines at the bottom of Windmill Brae. The Friday market at Aberdeen's Green can be seen in the distance in this 1948 picture.

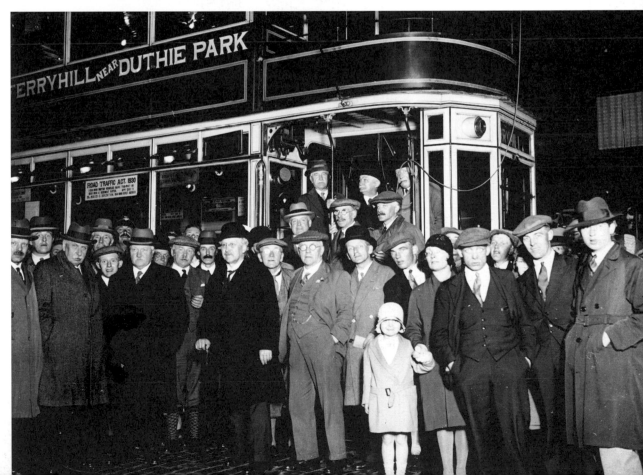

A souvenir picture to mark the last run of the Ferryhill tram in May 1931. The route ran from Aberdeen's Market Street and was laid in 1903.

An ancient flag-
stoned close, running
on to Aberdeen's
Broad Street, frames
this picture of the
demolition work in
January 1964

CHANGES

The end of an era as Broad Street buildings are demolished in January 1964. This area was earmarked for a car park for councillors and council officials.

CHAPTER TEN

CHANGES

NOTHING stands still in a city. Buildings come and go and boundaries expand. And all the changes are not necessarily for the better. Citizens of Aberdeen can complain about the worst excesses of building in the Sixties and Seventies, but we just had to put up with it – at least for a time.

Fortunately, the structures of this era lacked the solidity of earlier ages and are already disappearing, giving a new generation of town planners the chance to improve the appearance of the city.

The demolition of the ancient Castlehill Barracks was certainly a necessity in an era when slum housing was being replaced. But there are many buildings which citizens were sad to lose. When the Astoria fell to the wrecker's ball, a fine cinema and important meeting place was lost.

Then we have the pictorial record of the remarkable feat of moving a 360-year-old building, brick by brick, from the centre of town to Tillydrone. The preservation of the Wallace Tower showed a commitment to preserving the city's heritage that is commendable, although the tower is no longer the attraction it was in the centre of town. However, on this occasion, the construction of a superstore did not lead to the total loss of a historic legacy.

Other changes have come about inexorably altering the small events of our lives. The milkman with his clattering bottles and leather pouch for the weekly payments. The postmen in their old-style uniforms. The steam rollers which were such a source of fascination for young and old alike.

In this section there's a chance to relive those days.

Buildings are cleared from
Aberdeen's Netherkirkgate
in February 1964.

Provost Skene's House stands secure as the newer houses that surrounded it are razed in 1964.

A workman holds his head in his hands as part of a tenement building crashes down the wrong way in January 1964. The fifty-foot-high building was meant to fall into the car park on Broad Street but partially crashed into the street just missing the windows of a furniture store.

The Astoria Cinema, Kittybrewster, Aberdeen, is knocked down in April 1967. It opened in 1934 and was one of only two cinemas in the city to boast a theatre organ.

Part of the Castlehill Barracks site in Aberdeen is cleared.

The last vestiges of a military history stretching back to the 1650s are razed at Castlehill. Originally, a fort commanding the harbour stood on the site before the depot of the Gordon Highlanders was built in later years. It was in 1935 that the Gordons marched from the barracks for the last time.

Demolition work at part of the
site of Castlehill Barracks in
November 1965. The area was
associated with the military
from Cromwellian times up to
1935. The site was being cleared
for the building of the multi-
storey block of flats, which now
dominates the area behind the
Salvation Army Citadel.

A corner of the former Castlehill
Barracks is demolished in 1965.

The ancient Netherkirkgate in Aberdeen, as work begins on the Marks & Spencer store in 1964. In the background is the Wallace Tower, which stood alone on that spot when it was built as part of a townhouse for Sir Robert Keith of Benholm around 1600.

The new skyline is shaped. A skyscraper under construction in 1962.

The Wallace Tower, with its statue of an unknown knight in a niche, is dismantled in February 1964. The name most likely derives from Well House, which the building was known as in the nineteenth century.

Plans for the reconstruction of the Wallace Tower are studied as the tower begins to take shape again.

The Wallace Tower, also known as Benholm's Lodging, is painstakingly reconstructed at Tillydrone in June 1964 after the stones of the building were transported from the city centre.

The Marks & Spencer building in Aberdeen under construction on St Nicholas Street in August 1965.

Aberdeen's St Nicholas Street in 1965 before the St Nicholas and Bon Accord shopping centres straddled the area. The St Nicholas Centre dates from 1985 and the Bon Accord Centre from 1990. They brought a new shopping experience to the city.

The tram rails are removed from Union Street, Aberdeen, across from the up-for-sale Northern Club and YMCA buildings in 1958. The Northern Club members had moved to their new premises at Albyn Place in 1955.

The tram rails on Pittodrie Street, Aberdeen, are lifted in 1960.

Aberdeen's Auchinyell Bridge under construction in August 1960.

Springfield Road under construction
in Aberdeen, 1960.

Workmen constructing Aberdeen's
Springfield Road on 29 November
1960. Craigiebuckler Church can be
seen in the background.

Two men climb Ogston's soap works chimney in the Gallowgate, Aberdeen, on 16 November 1959, as it is prepared for demolition. It was the beginning of the end of the 200-foot-high landmark in Loch Street. The chimney was a remnant of the once-thriving Ogston soap factory, which was destroyed during the Second World War.

A factory chimneystack is brought crashing down during demolition work at Johnshaven in 1950.

The Logie Buchan ferry across the River Ythan in the 1930s. The ferry was replaced by a bridge built as a war memorial for the men of the parish who died in the First World War.

Driver William Ritchie prepares to take the road roller, affectionately known as Little Jocky, on her final journey out of Aberdeen County Council's Bucksburn roads depot to the breakers' yard at Port Elphinstone in 1962.

Old steamroller Little Jocky is taken on its last journey in Aberdeen, 29 January 1962.

The village postie at Whinnyfold, near Cruden Bay, collecting mail in 1961.

It's a long road to travel for postman Howie Kellas at Strathdon in 1962, serving the remotest of homes. Here, Howie closes a sheep barrier at Mains of Glencarvie. He delivered mail to the remote homesteads at the head of the glen from 1937. In 1962, he got this Land Rover to make the job a lot easier.

Old and new transport for delivering milk, 10 January 1950. The Kennerty milk deliveries in Aberdeen were being, at least partially, motorised.

A Kennerty Dairy milk cart on its rounds in Aberdeen in 1950.

Nearing the end of the milk round in Aberdeen's West End on a January morning in 1962. The leather satchel over the shoulder of the milkman indicates he is collecting weekly payments from customers as well as delivering milk.

An electric battery-powered van piled with milk crates at Mid Stocket, Aberdeen, in 1963.

REGAL JOURNEY

QUEEN Victoria's Aberdeen night flit was a well-organised affair. It had to be. Taking a heavy bronze statue from its plinth and moving it along the city's main thoroughfare was no easy task.

   The bronze of the Empress had been at the corner of St Nicholas Street and Union Street from 1893 when it replaced a marble statue erected at that spot in 1866. That statue can now be seen in Aberdeen Town House.

A close view of the bronze statue of Queen Victoria in 1964 at the Corner of St Nicholas Street.

The corner of Aberdeen's St Nicholas Street and Union Street as it was in January 1964 with Queen Victoria's statue presiding over the scene. The imposing entrance of the former New Market can be seen on Market Street.

Crowds look on as a crane prepares
to lift Queen Victoria from her
plinth to transport her to Queen's
Cross on 21 January 1964.

Up, up and away. The statue of Queen
Victoria leaves her plinth at
St Nicholas Street, Aberdeen, after
more than seventy years.

Workmen and engineers
put the finishing touches to
enthroning Queen Victoria
at Queen's Cross looking
towards Balmoral.

Wind breaks are much in evidence in this 1962 scene at Montrose Beach.

LEISURE

A summer scene at Montrose seafront in 1962 when most people took their holidays at home rather than abroad.

CHAPTER ELEVEN

LEISURE

IN the post-Second World War era, people would take the benefit of their newly-won trade fortnight holidays at home. In those days, Aberdonians might consider a day trip to Tarlair Lido, or a week in Montrose.

I have fond memories of holidays in Kirriemuir and can recall when my sister sent holiday postcards from Stonehaven. These pictures from that era may prompt some happy memories from the age before jet travel and foreign holidays for the masses.

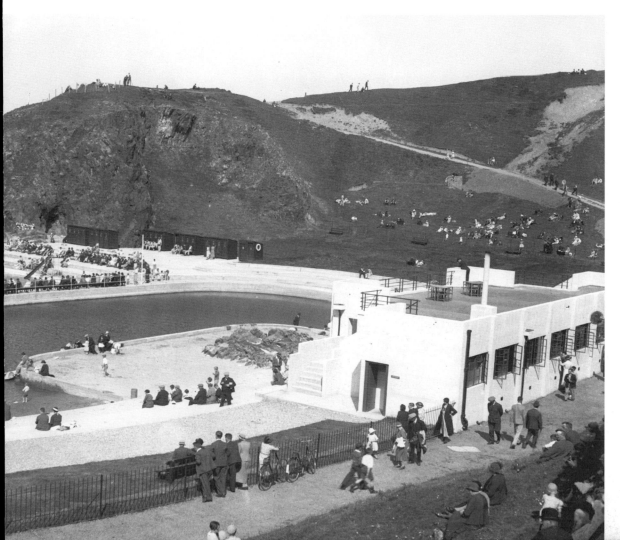

The Tarlair Lido near Macduff in 1936. The swimming pool had opened the previous summer with concrete terracing, paddling pool pavilion, tearoom, changing rooms and diving boards. Carved from a natural cove, it had twin pools and was the result of the vision of James Hird, who swam in Salmon Howe, close to the Howe of Tarlair. In 1897, he realized it was an ideal site for a pool and, when he became a member of Macduff Town Council, started fund raising events to fund the project. After twenty-five years, his efforts were repaid when the Town Council took up the scheme and burgh surveyor John Miller, who had worked on pool construction at North Berwick, planned the charming art deco lido amid the rocks. Sadly, it has fallen out of use.

Rubislaw Quarry, the 465-foot-deep hole that gave up the granite to give Aberdeen its unique appearance.

MEN OF GRANITE

Quarry manager John Ross and Robert Murison
measure a great block of granite on the 465-foot-
deep floor of Rubislaw Quarry in 1964.

CHAPTER TWELVE

MEN OF GRANITE

THE history of the North-east is built on solid foundations.

One of the key figures in building its reputation as granite supplier to the world was John Fyfe, who took over the family quarrying business at Tyrebagger, just outside Aberdeen, when his father died. John was only sixteen years old. Despite his youth, he was a formidable and enterprising businessman and by the age of twenty-four, was the foremost in his trade.

However, it was when he started his operations at Kemnay Quarry that the world began to learn of John Fyfe.

Although the advances of steam engineering and the opening of the Alford Valley Railway made Kemnay a viable site for Fyfe's operations in the quarry itself, the granite was hard won from the earth with manual labour. But by the 1860s, the resourceful John Fyfe was working with Andrew Barclay of Kilmarnock to produce the steam derrick crane and revolutionise quarrying. His most famous innovation was the Blondin Cableway, an aerial ropeway crane named after the famous high-wire performer of the day. This could lift large rocks from the floor of a quarry.

A tireless advocate of the advantages of granite, John Fyfe was quick to take affront if building work in Aberdeen used any other material. To ensure the historic bridge linking Aberdeen to Torry was built of granite, he slashed thousands of pounds off the lowest cost estimate.

Other buildings in Aberdeen that stand testimony to his energy in promoting granite are Marischal College, the Central Library, His Majesty's Theatre and the former main Post Office.

Kemnay Quarry produced stone for structures around the world. The Cenotaph, Tower Bridge and Thames Embankment in London, the Forth Railway Bridge and the Sydney Opera House are some of the more famous.

John Fyfe died in 1903, and the firm has changed hands many times, but his name lives on in the famous Fyfestone masonry blocks that continue to be prized by architects. The exact mix remains a secret but it includes natural North-east granite aggregates.

Kemnay Quarry ceased work in 1996 although there was a special blasting in 2000 to provide granite for the Scottish Parliament.

Kemnay Quarry in 1946. It was opened by John Fyfe in 1858. When the quarry operation started, Kemnay was just a scattering of crofts and cottages on the banks of the River Don.

Granite workers, some with pneumatic drills, at work in Kemnay Quarry in 1946. It was in that year that it saw one of the biggest quarry blasts ever carried out in the north of Scotland. Using three-and-a-half tons of explosives, 50,000 tons of rock was blasted from the quarry walls, falling 300ft to the floor. The explosives were laid in three channels up to 50ft long and 100ft from the top of the quarry.

Looking down hundreds of feet to the floor of Rubislaw Quarry when it was still a going concern.

Two men at work shaping a huge slab of granite blasted from the walls of Rubislaw Quarry.

Rubislaw Quarry, the 465-foot-deep hole that gave up the granite to give Aberdeen its unique appearance. Quarrying work began in 1740 and ended in 1971, in which time some six million tons of rock was extracted. In 2010, the quarry went on the market with a price tag of £30,000 and was acquired by two Aberdeen businessmen. The five-acre quarry has now filled with water. This picture was taken in 1964 when there was still extraction work.

Huge slabs of rock await attention after a blasting operation at Rubislaw Quarry.

After nearly 200 years of quarrying, this was the Rubislaw site in 1937.

Lifting a granite block at Rubislaw Quarry, Aberdeen, in the 1950s.

A diamond-tipped saw gets to work reducing the raw stone to more manageable sizes in 1965. This multi-blade gang saw, with diamond-impregnated blades, was the only one of its kind in Aberdeen when it came into operation. The saw could cut at the rate of six inches (15cm) an hour.

A worker with a granite saw in Aberdeen.

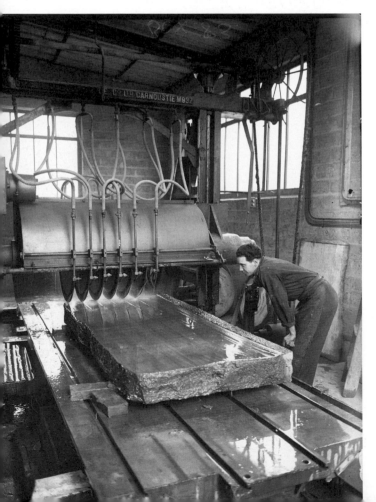

Multiple saws cutting granite at the workshops in the Charles McDonald Granite Yard in the 1950s.

Laying the road at Aberdeen Harbour
with granite setts.

A pneumatic drill takes up the granite
setts, or cassies as they are known in
Aberdeen, as the tram lines on Union
Terrace are raised in 1955. Note the empty
site at the corner of Bridge Street and
Union Street where the Palace Hotel stood
until this landmark building burned down.

Fashioning granite setts for the roads around 1934.

Workmen at a Hopeman, Moray, sandstone quarry in 1963.

Workers on the long climb up from the floor of Kemnay Quarry in 1946. The granite not only gives Aberdeen its Silver City tag, but also lends style and solidity to the Thames Embankment and the piers of Tower Bridge, London, and other locations across the UK and the world. Granite from Kemnay is also used in the Scottish Parliament building in Edinburgh. Workers who learned their trade in the North-east emigrated to spread their skills across the world and helped develop the industry, particularly in the US.

Many workshops sprang up throughout Aberdeen to meet the worldwide demand for dressed granite. Here, a workman is preparing a piece of granite for a customer.

The heavy work of chipping a granite slab into shape in 1966.

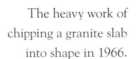

Early morning activity at the fish market in the Sixties.

FISHING FOLK

Two children take more interest in the cameraman than the work at hand as fish are hung up to dry on a frame at Collieston in 1935.

CHAPTER THIRTEEN

FISHING FOLK

NO photographic record of the North-east would be complete without a look at communities that sustained the area's great fishing trade.

Here we picture the fishing families baiting lines and repairing nets for what was little more than a cottage industry. In these images we show the bustling harbours of a business that had a profound impact on the North-east, bringing jobs and wealth for decades as it reached its zenith in the mid-twentieth century.

We also feature a ship that was at one time a familiar sight at the harbour and has a fascinating history.

Aberdeen Fish Market with early steam
trawlers lining the quayside.

Baiting fishing lines at Old
Torry, Aberdeen, in this picture
from the pre-steam days.

Fisher girls fill barrels at Aberdeen in the 1930s.

The fish huts at Fraserburgh, where travelling fisherwomen would stay.

An iced-up Regent Quay
at Aberdeen Harbour in
January 1963.

Unloading trawlers at
Aberdeen in the 1930s.

An Aberdeen Fish Market scene in the heyday of the steam trawler.

A fishwife at work in Old Torry outside the distinctive houses that have now all been swept away.

Net making at Buckie in 1935.

Gutting fish at sea on board the small vessel *Hazel* of Fraserburgh in 1965.

The coal boat *Spray* is unloaded at Aberdeen in 1966.

Preparing for the sales at Aberdeen Fish Market in 1962.

An aerial view of
Aberdeen Harbour
showing the basins and
fish market.

An aerial view of Aberdeen
Harbour from 1948 with
Fittie top left and bottom
right the dock gates, which
were built in 1897.

Aberdeen Harbour busy with
trawlers before the port became
more famous for oil supply ships
than fishing vessels.

Loading herring on to a lorry at Torry, Aberdeen, in 1964.

The *Aberdonian* lies at its berth at Aberdeen Harbour. This ship had a colourful career. Built on the Clyde in 1909, she was initially a passenger-carrying vessel, which at one time plied twice a week between Aberdeen and London. In the 1930s, the Aberdeen Steam Navigation Company said in its leaflets, "the accommodation for both First and Second Cabin passengers is very superior." The company adds: "Passengers who wish to do so may sleep on board in London – bed and breakfast 1st cabin, 7/6; 2nd cabin, 5/-." During the First World War, the *Aberdonian* served as a hospital ship. In the Second World War, she was a depot ship for coastal forces. Sold to new owners in 1946, the *Aberdonian* was renamed *Taishan Peak* and moved to Hong Kong. But the ship was damaged by a typhoon in 1948 and finally broken up in 1950.

The lights of the cargo vessel *Bruno* illuminate Aberdeen Harbour in 1953.

Men at work building the modern day seawall at Cullen.

A spectacular granary fire lights up the night sky at Aberdeen's Cotton Street as firemen fight to contain the flames in October 1963. Hundreds gathered on the Beach Boulevard to watch as the building, belonging to the North-eastern Agricultural Society, was destroyed. Several of the thirty-five firemen fighting the blaze had narrow escapes as burning debris fell from the roof and an elevator tower split and crashed to the ground. Firemaster W. H. Woods had to withdraw his men from inside the building because of the heat and smoke. He said: "There are hoppers which run from the top of the building to the bottom and my men had to feel their way around in case they fell."

DRAMAS

Fire consumes a tree as flames leap into a forest in April 1960.

CHAPTER FOURTEEN

DRAMAS

THE dramas that came to the North and North-east of Scotland always grabbed the prominent headlines. The bravery of the rescue services has long been celebrated, and deservedly so.

Outstanding among these heroes are the fire fighters. Whether it be a Deeside castle or a warehouse, the drama of controlling blazes and saving property has always commanded the public's attention.

The diversity of challenges facing fire fighters is shown here, from preserving priceless old artefacts to tackling blaze-stricken high-rise flats.

The dangers fire fighters confront daily are also brought home by one incident when part of a blazing building collapses with fire fighters inside it.

But in the cliff rescue we feature, it was not just the coastguard and fire services that were the lifesavers. In this instance, the public and reporters assisted in a difficult operation.

Sadly, in the Loch Ness tragedy with the speed record breaker John Cobb, nothing could be done after his jet boat hit ripples of water at high speed.

Crathes Castle on 6 January 1966 after a blaze swept through two wings of the Deeside landmark. Five people fled the fire in their nightclothes, two having to clamber down an escape ladder. The fire hit the Victorian and Queen Anne wings of the castle, which dates back to the sixteenth century. The medieval tower with its ornate ceilings and the priceless Horn of Leys, a gift to the Burnett family from King Robert the Bruce, were undamaged. The Burnett family upheld an ancient tradition by ensuring the jeweled horn was made safe before any other belongings. The castle and grounds, home to the Burnetts of Leys for over 350 years, is a National Trust for Scotland property.

The charred interior of Crathes
Castle after the 1966 blaze.

Precious furniture, paintings
and artefacts lie destroyed
after the Crathes fire.

A forest fire blots out the Deeside hills in April 1960.

There was a new challenge for firemen as high-rise flats started to appear in Aberdeen. In this scene from 1961, the fire fighters practice a rescue from a top-floor flat at Ashgrove multi-storey flats.

Fire fighters demonstrate how they would rescue residents from a multi-storey flat.

Aberdeen firemen douse a smouldering warehouse roof in 1959.

A fire tender stands by the trouble-hit coal boat *Ferryhill* at Aberdeen Harbour in June 1966. The Aberdeen collier had lain strikebound for three weeks after Aberdeen dockers refused to handle the cargo. But the danger of spontaneous combustion of the unworked coal had concerned the ship's officers and owners. Their fears were realised when smoke started coming from the several hundred tons of coal in the hold. The fire brigade were alerted and three fire units were ordered to the harbour to pump water into the hold and bring the problem under control.

RESCUE

Public rage over an attack on a woman sparked a campaign that ended in success when electric street lighting came to Hilton Place, Aberdeen, in 1966. Local people's annoyance at their dim gas-lit street turned to anger when a female student was attacked. This sparked a petition, which was sent to the council. One resident said that because streets around it had electric lighting, walking into Hilton Place was "like walking into a black tunnel". The new concrete lamp standard is seen next to an old gas lamp.

Police, coastguards, the Press and holidaymakers leant a hand in this July 1959 rescue at Gregness, south of Aberdeen. John Baillie, aged sixteen, took a fall while climbing on the 70ft cliff near a coastguard station. He was semi-conscious and lying beside the sea when he was reached. After he was hauled to the top of the cliff, an ambulance took the boy to hospital. He was not in a serious condition. Interestingly, the mishap prompted an article in *The Press and Journal* – not calling for a ban on climbing, but encouraging better judgment of risks.

JOHN COBB

WORLD land speed record holder John Cobb at the controls of the jet-engined *Crusader* on Loch Ness before his fateful attempt to set a new record on water. The hydroplane was thirty-one feet long and her de Havilland Ghost turbojet had 5,000 pounds of thrust.

John Cobb had reached 240mph on the measured mile on the Highland loch when the craft's nose dipped into the water and exploded into pieces. Cobb was hurled from the open cockpit but died of shock. The crash is believed to have been caused by three ripples from a timekeeper's boat.

Cobb was a big man, a quiet unassuming gentleman who won the hearts of the folk at Drumnadrochit during his preparations for the record attempt. Before his record attempt on that September day in 1952, he told his wife and his mother that he had a premonition about what became his last run. Thousands of people lined the streets of Inverness to bid farewell to John Cobb as his hearse left for Surrey.

Musicians get a big reception at a Fraserburgh rock and roll concert in 1956.

YOUTH ON
THE MOVE

Acrobatic dancers at Fraserburgh in October 1956.

CHAPTER FIFTEEN

YOUTH ON THE MOVE

UNTIL the 1940s, the word teenager was seldom used in our language and certainly not in the sense it is used today. It was not until 1944 that the *Encyclopaedia Britannica* introduced it as a new word.

That says much for the way youngsters were viewed then. The youth of the day were seen as going through a necessary but not very useful phase on the route to adulthood. Youngsters had little money and not much of a voice in society. The youth culture, which so dominates today, was undreamed of then. When it did come about, it was another of the many changes wrought in society by the World Wars.

As Britain, and the world, began to emerge from post-war austerity, youngsters began to assert themselves and form an identity. Youth culture was on the march.

Greater spending ability gave them real power. In an explosion of energy, youth asserted itself. Different clothes, different music, different attitudes arrived. From the university quadrangle to the work floor, little was to remain unchanged. And it was a change destined to just grow and grow.

It was in 1955 that Bill Haley and his Comets caused a sensation with the number 'Rock Around the Clock' after it was played over the opening credits of the film *Blackboard Jungle*. The song had been recorded the previous year, but it needed the exposure the film provided to make it an anthem for a youth revolution.

The film provoked widely reported riots in some British cinemas with seats broken and Teddy Boys jiving in the aisles. And the young in North-east Scotland rushed to adopt the clothes and dances inspired by rock and roll.

Protest was also a part of this radical change as students led the way in direct action to make political points over international and national causes.

Dancing couples in 1955.

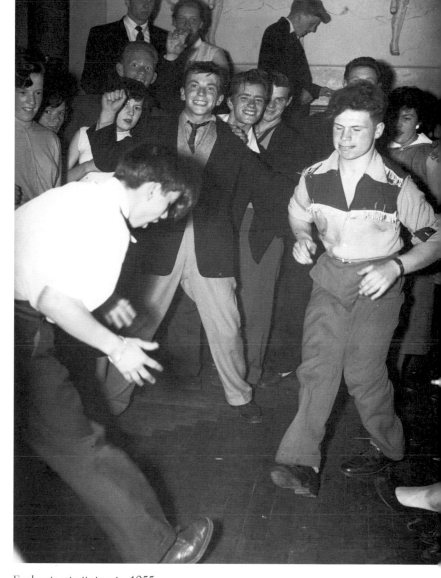

Enthusiastic jiving in 1955.

Jiving to rock and roll music at Fraserburgh in 1956.

Teddy Boys at a dance in North-east Scotland in 1955.

On 3 December 1969, the apartheid system of legal racial segregation in South Africa was one of the most toxic political issues. Emotions were high when the Springboks – on a controversial British tour – arrived in a snowy Aberdeen to play a North of Scotland select. An estimated 1,000 demonstrators marched to Linksfield Stadium where the rugby match was to take place. Here, a policeman wrestles protesters to the ground after a pitch invasion.

Apartheid protesters at Linksfield, now the Chris Anderson Stadium, are each accompanied by at least two policemen as they are taken to a temporary charge room. There were ninety-eight arrests at the Aberdeen match.

Students from Aberdeen at the House of Commons in 1976 lobbying MPs in support of student teachers facing unemployment when they complete their courses.

Aberdeen students hold a rally in the quad at Marischal College during a 1986 protest over the Government's latest round of cuts to grants and benefits.

This picture
shows the
enormity of the
job of digging out
a stranded train
at Newmachar
in January 1960.

STORMY WEATHER

A snow blower in action in the 1950s.

CHAPTER SIXTEEN

STORMY WEATHER

THE snowstorms of 1958 and 1960 stretched the rescue services and transport systems of the day to breaking point.

High winds whipped up blizzards that left people stranded in remote communities for days. Trains loaded with passengers were trapped and lines of traffic were caught in snowdrifts.

Rescuers didn't have the advantage of as much heavy snow shifting equipment as is now available but made up for it with hard manual labour.

These pictures remind us yet again that Mother Nature rules.

Hard-packed snow around the Aberdeen to Fraserburgh train, snowbound between Maud and Strichen for three days in 1958. When the stranded train's heating failed, four women from Fraserburgh trudged through snow to the shelter of nearby Viewbank farmhouse. One of the stranded women said: "We would never have been able to walk back to the relief train in yon snow." But after ninety railwaymen with a plough fought their way through to the farmhouse, the cheery women at last took the same route home as their thirty fellow passengers when the relief train was coupled to the carriages – but three days later.

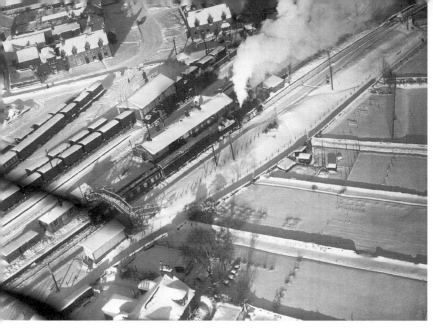

A stranded train at Maud Station, Aberdeenshire, victim of the heavy snows of January 1958.

The general scene at Blairton Inn after the great storm of January 1958, with a long line of lorries trapped in snow as they made their way to Aberdeen. This was one of the worst roadblocks in the area.

The passenger train stranded between Maud and Strichen from Wednesday, 22 January to Friday, 24 January 1958. The isolated farmhouse at Viewbank, bottom right of picture, gave refuge to passengers. This desolate scene shows how badly Buchan was hit by that blizzard.

The scene of a dramatic rescue when the Fraserburgh diesel train was trapped in snow drifts at Newmachar in January 1960. For fifty-seven passengers it was a sixteen-hour ordeal as a raging blizzard piled snow as high as the carriages. A gang of twenty railwaymen battled through ten-foot drifts in darkness to reach the Aberdeen-bound train. It was 4am when the passengers finally walked along a 500-yard path carved through the snow by their rescuers to reach a relief train.

Even the steam locomotive with the snowplough is brought to a halt as it tries to batter its way through to reach the snowbound Fraserburgh to Aberdeen train.

A train with a snowplough batters its way through high-piled snow to rescue passengers stranded at Newmachar by the blizzard of January 1960.

Smiles of relief from the passengers rescued from the train at Newmachar after they reached Aberdeen a day late. As they warmed themselves, they spoke of their ordeal. One passenger said the snow was so high "you could have poked a stick through the window right into the middle of it". Another passenger was eighteen-year-old bride-to-be Betty Grant of Peterhead who was on a trip to buy her wedding dress. "It was quite an experience," she said. "But I'm not looking on it as a bad omen."

The snow is close to covering the stranded Fraserburgh to Aberdeen train as men dig it free in 1960.

After the snowplough did its work and reached the train at Newmachar, there was the hard labour of digging it out.

The relief train can be seen on the right as men work to clear the
line between it and the snow-bound train at Newmachar.

The driver and fireman of the stranded train at Tillycorthie Bridge.

Men at work to free the stranded train at Tillycorthie Bridge, near Udny Station, in February 1960.

A bleak snow-covered landscape surrounds the stranded goods train at Tillycorthie Bridge near Udny in 1960. A locomotive fitted with a snowplough is approaching the trapped train.

A train passes a snowplough coming in the other direction at Gartly in March 1960

After the big snow of January 1960, a householder digs his way to his coal shed at Newmachar.

Newmachar Station with snow piled high in January 1960.

A snow blower in action in the blocked Glens of Foudland on the A96 in March 1965.

A column of snow streams from a snow blower fighting to clear a path through the Glens of Foudland in March 1965. Beside the blower is a lorry, which was stuck in the snow all night. Whole communities were cut off by this storm, made worse by winds gusting up to 60mph, which built up huge drifts and caused chaos on roads throughout Britain.

After the 1960 storm, lorries remain fast in snowdrifts at Newmachar.

A snowy scene from December 1961, showing a milk lorry being loaded.

Making the most of a decent snow covering at the Devil's Elbow in 1961. The steep double hairpin bend on the old road through Gleann Beag at the Cairnwell pass has now been bypassed, but was a challenge for motorists in days when cars were not as powerful or reliable as they are today. The Glenshee area, rising above 2,000ft beside the Devil's Elbow, was first used by skiers in the 1930s with its popularity growing over the following decades.

Snowy conditions did not deter this milk cart in Aberdeen in November 1965. At the reins is Hugh Will, a well-known "milko" who retired in 1965. His premises on the Great Northern Road were demolished to make way for the dual carriageway.

Large crowds make use of the Glenshee snow-covered slopes and chairlift.

The growth of skiing led to the development of a ski centre at Glenshee in the early 1960s. Here, large crowds enjoy the Glenshee facilities in 1985.

Representatives of the Boys' Brigade march past the Queen and Duke of Edinburgh at Balmoral Castle to mark the movement's anniversary.

ROYAL DAYS

The flags are out for Princess Margaret's visit to open the new Fraserburgh Academy in 1962.
The town's entire school population of 2,000 gathered in the playground to welcome Princess
Margaret and Lord Snowdon.

CHAPTER SEVENTEEN

ROYAL DAYS

THE Queen and Duke of Edinburgh helped celebrate the seventy-fifth anniversary of the Boys' Brigade on 6 September 1958.

Representatives of the BB went on parade at Balmoral Castle and showed their appreciation of the Monarch's interest with rousing cheers.

In September 1962, Buchan had a Royal day to celebrate when Princess Margaret and Lord Snowdon visited Fraserburgh and Peterhead.

The children who lined the streets with flags had even more to cheer about when the Princess requested an extra day's holiday for the pupils after opening the new Fraserburgh Academy.

Children line up outside Fraserburgh's new academy waiting for the Royal couple to arrive to officially open the impressive new building.

A smile and sympathy from the Queen as she hands a Queen's Badge to Boys' Brigade Cpl C. M. Robertson of Aberdeen as he stands to attention despite his plastered leg.

Three cheers for the Queen. Caps are raised by BB members at a Balmoral reception to mark their seventy-fifth anniversary.

A large crowd gathered in flag-bedecked Peterhead on 20 September 1962 to catch a glimpse of Princess Margaret and Lord Snowdon when they visited the town. The Princess opened a new maternity wing at the Cottage Hospital and the couple visited the South Harbour where they were shown round the fishing vessel Faithful. When they reached the harbour, the Royal couple were greeted by cheers and the hooting of sirens on the decorated boats of the fishing fleet.

Sir Harry Lauder, one of Scotland's most famous entertainers, at the unveiling of a bronze bust on the grave of James Scott Skinner in 1931. Scott Skinner was the self-styled Strathspey King. His distinctive fiddle music was a favourite of royalty and he drew huge audiences during his long career. The Banchory-born master musician wrote over 600 fiddle tunes based on the Deeside music he learned as a child. More than 40,000 people lined the streets of Aberdeen as James Scott Skinner's cortege passed on its way to Allenvale Cemetery in 1927.

FAME AND CELEBRITY

The Aberdeen and District Dairy Queen
of 1960 poses after her win.

CHAPTER EIGHTEEN

FAME AND CELEBRITY

THE easy celebrity of our mass media world was not available to the notable figures in an earlier era. It took long decades tramping the boards in theatres and music halls around the country before artists became part of the national consciousness.

The lasting fame of people like James Scott Skinner and Sir Harry Lauder was all the more remarkable for that. They enjoyed true fame, very different from the easily achieved stardom of the twenty-first century.

For the boxer Benny Lynch, his fame came at a high price. The Scot was a boxing sensation both sides of the Atlantic but his descent from the giddy heights of adulation was swift and tragic.

But we can all share in the obvious delight of the Dairy Queen of 1960 and her moment in the spotlight.

The Dairy Queen and Princess of 1960 head off on a BEA flight after gaining their titles.

Scotland's first world boxing champion, Benny Lynch, at a boxing booth at Aberdeen Beach in 1938. Benny was only twenty-one when he beat Jackie Brown to take the world flyweight title in 1935. But by 1938, his drinking lifestyle was taking its toll and when he failed to make the weight for a flyweight defence, he lost his world title. On 3 October of that same year, Lynch suffered the only knockout of his professional career. His fighter's licence was revoked and he suffered a rapid decline into alcoholism and penury. The boxer from the Glasgow Gorbals was just thirty-three when he died. On this visit to Aberdeen, he was matched against Freddie Tennant, a top-class Dundee fighter and one time Scottish champion. He faced Lynch in the ring five times, managing a victory and a draw. The boxing booth was run by Tom Wood, pictured centre. The travelling booths were hugely popular in the pre-war years, attracting world-class fighters and paying good money in those austere times.

Fraserburgh players in their dressing room celebrating defeating Dundee in the first-round of the Scottish Cup.

SPORTING LIFE

Despite their heroics in the Scottish Cup of 1959, when they knocked out Dundee in the
first round, Fraserburgh fell to Stirling Albion in a seven-goal thriller in the next round.
Here, Broch beat the Stirling keeper.

Chapter Nineteen

SPORTING LIFE

THE greatest day in Fraserburgh Football Club's history – a history which stretches back to 1894 – came on 31 January 1959, at their Bellslea Park home ground.

When the Highland League Club lined up against the high-flying stars of Dundee in the first round of the Scottish Cup, few outside the Broch gave them much of a chance.

Even when wee Johnny Strachan headed home in the forty-forth minute from a George Brander corner, it was expected that the Dundee side, with its Scottish international players, would put the Highland upstarts in their place.

But desperate Dundee pressure failed to put the ball past keeper Danny Mowat and the game ended with amazing scenes of celebration from the Fraserburgh fans.

Johnny Strachan was the local hero who scored the goal to knock Dundee out of the Scottish Cup in 1959.

Goal-mouth pressure from Fraserburgh during the momentous 1959 Scottish Cup clash with Dundee.

Bellslea Park is crammed with fans of the Highland League club as Johnny Strachan scores a minute before half-time. It was one of Dundee's most embarrassing defeats. Stirling Albion defeated the Broch side in the next round but the ripples caused by the Cup upset were such that the Scottish League changed the contest rules the next season preventing Highland League clubs meeting Scottish League clubs in the preliminary rounds.

LIGHTING THE PITCH

THE Scottish obsession with football has remained unchanged and undiminished over the decades. While the simple drama of team pitted against team remains as enthralling as ever, the experience of watching a game has changed hugely.

Young fans of the present era will not remember the days when evening games were not possible. But it is just over fifty years ago that evening games came to Pittodrie Stadium. That first floodlit match against Luton Town ushered in an era that saw massive changes in the experience of the fan. Terracings were eventually to give way to all-seater stadiums, essential safety measures were enacted and under-soil heating was introduced to counteract our harsh winters. All elements that went to make modern-day football the spectacle it is.

The view over the home of Aberdeen Football Club from the top of a 120-foot-high floodlight pylon in 1959. Lord Provost George Stephen gave the signal to switch on the lights for the first time and described the event as "quite an occasion in the history of Aberdeen FC".

A pylon for floodlights is erected at Pittodrie Stadium. The game that heralded the era of nighttime games took place on 22 October 1959, and was against Luton Town. A crowd of 16,000 turned out to see the Dons beat the English Cup finalists of the previous season 3-2. Aberdeen's Hugh Baird was judged to be one of the stars of the evening.

In 1971, theatregoers in Aberdeen were treated to a show that was a roll call of the top Scottish performers. In this line-up are Anne and Laura Brand, The Corries, George Chisholm, Rikki Fulton, John Grieve, Kenneth McKellar, Jack Milroy, The New Faces, Danny Street, The Alex Welsh Jazz Band, Moira Anderson, The Karlins, Jimmy Logan, Lena Martell, Chic Murray, Jimmy Shand, Ian Wallace, and the Shotts and Dykehead Pipe Band.

CURTAIN UP

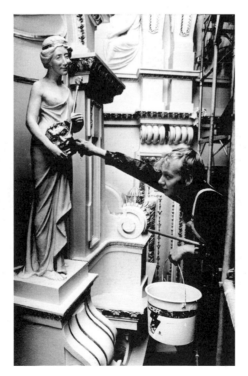

The mask of comedy in the arms of the
statue of comedy, high on the wall of His
Majesty's Theatre, gets cleaned in 1987.

Chapter Twenty

CURTAIN UP

HIS Majesty's Theatre has had a special place in the hearts of Aberdonians since it opened its doors for the first time more than 100 years ago.

HMT remains a landmark in the city centre, but one that has always kept up with the times and never allowed changes in the world of entertainment to leave it behind.

All tastes are catered for yearly, from ballet and musicals to plays and variety. Children, youngsters and adults are all accommodated.

Here, we may bring back a few memories with these pictures from yesteryear.

The daunting job of painting His Majesty's Theatre was undertaken in a renovation that took two years. Here two of the seven-man team of painters are working 55ft above the floor of the theatre in 1982. The facelift cost £3 million.

Disappointed crowds outside His Majesty's after learning that Andy Stewart's show was cancelled. This is September 1964 and the singer had contracted laryngitis. Manager James Donald can be seen at the theatre's main entrance telling Andy's fans the bad news

His Majesty's Theatre is open again in 1982 after what Buff Hardie referred to as a "£3 million lick o' paint". The appropriately named opening show, *Curtains Up*, featured Scotland the What? with Buff Hardie, Stephen Robertson and George Donald, singers Patti Boulaye and Bill McCue, ventriloquist Ward Allen and dancers from the Scottish Ballet.

Comedian Rikki Fulton showed another aspect of his talents when he appeared at His Majesty's Theatre in 1986 in his own distinctive adaptation of a play by the French dramatist Molière. The actor, famous for his droll Rev. I. M. Jolly, is pictured with his wife Kate Matheson who was a Grampian TV presenter. The couple met when Ricki was appearing at the theatre. Cast members pictured are (from left) Iain Stuart Robertson, Ian Arthur, Joan Knight, director, Alan Vicary and Rebecca Hawking

Since the theatre opened in 1906, it's doubtful anyone can remember when William Wallace's statue stood before the rising edifice of Aberdeen's new Frank Matcham designed theatre.

When *Snow White* came to His Majesty's Theatre in 1986, there had to be a name change. Disney carefully guards its copyright so Doc, Sleepy, Grumpy, Dopey, Bashful, Happy and Sneezy became Pops, Snoozy, Surly, Dozy, Blusher, Jolly and Wheezy. Honor Blackman, who played the wicked queen, Ted Rogers: narrator, and Jane Arden: Snow White, are pictured with the seven renamed actors.

The year is 1970 and Andy Stewart proudly presents some of the cast of his new show at His Majesty's Theatre. That year The Brotherhood, Ron Dale, Sidney Devine and the Bruce McClure Dancers were among the entertainers. In 1970, dress circle tickets were 15/-, orchestra stalls 12/- 6d and you could get a private box for £3 3/-.

High above the stage at His Majesty's Theatre a "flyman" skilfully co-ordinates the raising and lowering of scenery and the curtain. With only buzzers or cue lights to help him, the "flyman" manipulates the ropes – around one and a half miles of them – to whisk scenery up or down. This picture dates from 1969.